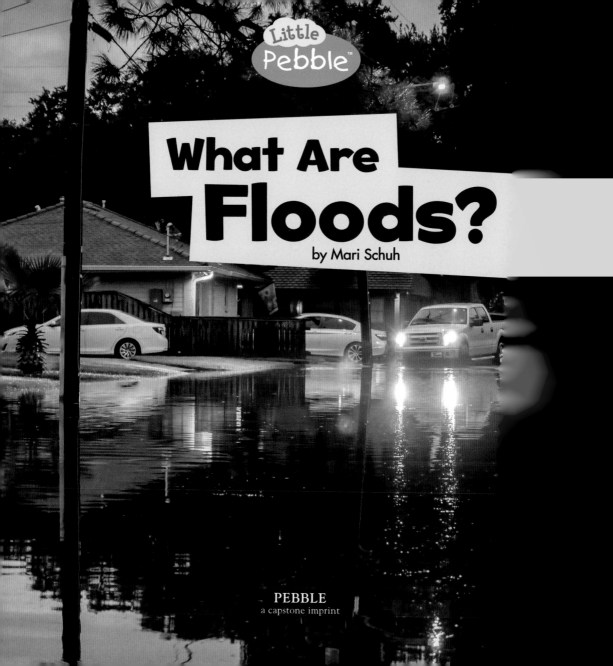

Little Pebble™

What Are
Floods?

by Mari Schuh

PEBBLE
a capstone imprint

Little Pebble is published by Pebble
1710 Roe Crest Drive, North
Mankato, Minnesota 56003
www.mycapstone.com

Library of Congress Cataloging-in-Publication Data
Names: Schuh, Mari C., 1975–author.
Title: What are floods? / by Mari Schuh.
Description: North Mankato, Minnesota : Pebble, a
   Capstone imprint, [2019] | Series: Little pebble.
   Wicked weather | Audience: Ages 4–8.
Identifiers: LCCN 2018029834 (print) | LCCN
   2018031694 (ebook) | ISBN 9781977103383
   (eBook PDF) | ISBN 9781977103314 (hardcover) |
   ISBN 9781977105486 (paperback)
Subjects: LCSH: Floods—Juvenile literature.
Classification: LCC GB1399 (ebook) | LCC GB1399 .S38
   2019 (print) | DDC 551.48/9—dc23
LC record available at https://lccn.loc.gov/2018029834

Editorial Credits
Nikki Potts, editor; Kyle Grenz, designer;
Heather Mauldin, media researcher; Tori Abraham, production specialist

Photo Credits
Getty Images: Orlando Sentinel, 21, Warren Faidley, 11; iStockphoto:
BanksPhotos, 7, 9, Philartphace, 17, sfe-co2, 1, skodonnell, 19; Shutterstock:
Augustin Lazaroiu, 13, Diachuk Vasyl, cover, Echunder, 15, thanatphoto, 5

Printed and bound in China.
000966

Table of Contents

What Is a Flood? 4

Staying Safe 16

Glossary 22
Read More 23
Internet Sites 23
Critical Thinking Questions . . 24
Index 24

What Is a Flood?

The water rises.

It does not stop.

It is a flood!

Lots of rain can cause floods.

Rivers fill up with water.

They overflow.

Look!

The dam broke.

Water rushes out.

The area floods.

dam

Hurricanes can cause floods.

Water covers the land.

Watch out!

A flash flood is fast!
It happens in a few hours
or less.

flash flood

A flood is strong.

Cars get swept away!

Crops are hurt.

Staying Safe

People work as a team.

Sandbags are put near water.

They help keep water away.

People make storm kits.

They see storm updates on TV.

They are ready!

People move to

higher ground.

Then they wait.

They go home when it is safe.

Glossary

crop—a plant farmers grow in large amounts, usually for food; farmers grow crops such as corn, soybeans, and peas

dam—a wall that stretches across a river; dams slow down the rushing water behind it

flash flood—a flood that happens with little or no warning, often during times of heavy rainfall

hurricane—a strong, swirling wind and rain storm that starts on the ocean; hurricanes are also called typhoons or cyclones

overflow—to spill over

storm kit—a container filled with food, water, flashlights, and other items that help people during a storm

Read More

Black, Vanessa. *Floods*. Disaster Zone. Minneapolis: Jump! Inc., 2017.

Johnson, Robin. *What Is a Flood?* Severe Weather Close-Up. New York: Crabtree Publishing Company, 2016.

Schuetz, Kristin. *Severe Weather*. Understanding Weather. Minneapolis: Bellwether Media, 2016.

Internet Sites

Use FactHound to find Internet sites related to this book.

Visit www.facthound.com

Just type in 9781977103314 and go.

Super-cool stuff!

Check out projects, games and lots more at
www.capstonekids.com

Critical Thinking Questions

1. How does a flood happen?

2. Name two ways people can get ready for a flood.

3. Why are floods dangerous?

Index

cars, 14

crops, 14

dams, 8

flash floods, 12

hurricanes, 10

rain, 6

rivers, 6

sandbags, 16

storm kits, 18

TV, 18